# Writing Paragraphs

Illustrated by Danny Beck

ISBN #1-56175-467-6

©1983, 1996 Remedia Publications. All rights reserved. Printed in the United States of America. The purchase of this book entitles the individual to reproduce copies for classroom use. The reproduction of any part for an entire school or school system or for commercial use is strictly prohibited.

**REMEDIA PUBLICATIONS**     **10135 E. VIA LINDA, #D124**     **SCOTTSDALE, AZ 85258**

# To The Teacher:

The pages in this book are designed to help students understand paragraphs and to encourage them to become better writer-communicators.

They will learn to develop topic sentences, arrange ideas in logical order, and add details to expand paragraphs.

## Answer Key

**Page 1** basketball, no   Cross out: People like to play baseball.   holes-in-one, no
Cross Out: People like to wear golf shoes.

**Page 2** pasta, no   Cross Out: Most people enjoy eating hamburgers.   cats, no
Cross Out: Dogs make good pets.

**Page 3 - Page 6** Answers will vary.

**Page 7** We live in a salty world.   The Blue Jay is not friendly with other birds.

**Page 8** Giant ships with sails are called clippers.   The last dinosaur died about 65 million years ago.

**Page 9 - Page 12** Answers will vary.

**Page 13** 1. The rocket blasted off. It traveled through space. It landed on the moon.

2. There was a snowstorm. The ground was covered with snow. The sun melted the snow.

3. Tony put on his parachute. He jumped out of the airplane. Tony landed safely.

4. We went to the restaurant. We ordered hamburgers. We ate dinner.

**Page 14** 1. The score of the game was tied. I hit a home run. We won the game.

2. Dark clouds appeared. It rained all afternoon. We played in the puddles.

3. The tire was flat. Tony got his air pump. He pumped air into the tire. Tony rode away on his bike.

4. Pat blew into the balloon. The balloon began to get big. The balloon got bigger and bigger. The balloon popped.

**Page 15** 1. Tim put a worm on the fishhook. 2. He threw the line into the water. 3. Tim caught a fish. 4. Then he cooked it.

**Page 16** 1. Rosa's phone rang. 2. She picked up the receiver. 3. She listened carefully. 4. She became very excited when she heard she had won a prize.

**Page 17 - Page 30** Answers will vary.

Writing Paragraphs ©1983, 1996 Remedia Publications

Name _____

# The Paragraph

A paragraph is one or more sentences that tell about one idea or thing. The first word in a paragraph is always indented. This means that it starts a little to the right of the left-hand margin.

**Read the paragraph below.**

Basketball is an American game. It was invented in America. The first basketball team had nine players. The first baskets were made from peach baskets. People like to play baseball.

**What is the paragraph about? Underline the correct answer.**
Americans       baseball       basketball       people

**Do all the sentences in the paragraph tell about the same thing?** ☐ Yes  ☐ No

**Cross out any sentence in the paragraph above that does not fit.**

**Read this paragraph.**

Some lucky golfers get the ball in the hole with the first shot. It's called a "hole-in-one." People like to wear golf shoes. There are more than you think. In 1979, there were 30,000 holes-in-one reported!

**What is the paragraph about? Underline the correct answer.**
1979       shoes       tennis       holes-in-one

**Do all the sentences tell about the same thing?** ☐ Yes  ☐ No

**Cross out any sentence in the paragraph above that does not fit.**

**Challenge: Choose one of the paragraphs above and write it correctly.**

© 1983, 1996 Remedia Publications                Writing Paragraphs

Name _____

# The Paragraph

**Read the paragraph below.**

    Do you like to eat pasta? Pasta means dough. You might call it spaghetti or macaroni. Pasta comes in 100 shapes. Some are shells. Others are wide noodles. Most people enjoy eating hamburgers. Pasta must be boiled until it is soft.

**What is the paragraph about? Underline the correct answer.**
    sauce      macaroni      pasta      lunch

**Do all the sentences in the paragraph tell about the same thing?** ☐ Yes ☐ No

**Cross out any sentence in the paragraph above that does not fit.**

**Read this paragraph.**

    For almost 5,000 years, cats have been kept as pets. Cats have a great sense of smell. They can't see as well as people, though. Whiskers help them feel their way in the dark. Dogs make good pets. Kittens' eyes open within two weeks of birth.

**What is the paragraph about? Underline the correct answer.**
    pets    cats    dogs    smelling

**Do all the sentences tell about the same thing?** ☐ Yes ☐ No

**Cross out any sentence in the paragraph above that does not fit.**

**Challenge: Choose one of the paragraphs above and write it correctly.**

Name _____

# Write About Yourself

> **An easy way to write a paragraph is to answer questions. When you write a few sentences about the same thing, you'll soon have a paragraph.**

**Write a complete sentence to answer each question.**

**ABOUT YOU**

1. What is your name?
2. How old are you?
3. When is your birthday?
4. Where do you live?
5. What school do you attend?
6. What grade are you in?

_____

_____
_____
_____
_____
_____
_____
_____
_____
_____
_____

**Make up a title for your paragraph.**

**Challenge:** Write four sentences about your family.

Name _____

# Write About a Friend

**Write a complete sentence to answer each question.**

### A FRIEND

1. What is your friend's name?
2. What does your friend look like?
3. How long have you been friends?
4. Where did you meet your friend?
5. What is one thing you especially like about your friend?
6. What is another thing you like about your friend?

**Make up a title for your paragraph.**

**Challenge:** Add another sentence to your paragraph.

Writing Paragraphs

Name _____

# Write About Your Favorite Place to Eat

**Write a complete sentence to answer each question.**

### FAVORITE PLACE TO EAT

1. What is the name of your favorite place to eat?
2. Why do you like to eat there?
3. What do you usually order?
4. How often do you eat there?
5. When was the last time you ate there?
6. Who usually goes with you?

_____

_____

_____
_____
_____
_____
_____
_____
_____
_____

**Make up a title for your paragraph.**

**Challenge:** Write four sentences about your favorite food.

© 1983, 1996 Remedia Publications

Name _____

# Write About a Robot

**Write a complete sentence to answer each question.**

### A HELPFUL ROBOT

1. What would be your robot's name?
2. How would the robot help you?
3. What other things could your robot do?
4. What would it look like?
5. Where would your robot live?
6. Would you share your robot with others?

**Make up a title for your paragraph.**

**Challenge: Add another sentence to your paragraph.**

Name _____

# The Topic Sentence

> **Every paragraph has a main idea or topic sentence.**
> **This tells what the paragraph is about.**
> **The topic sentence usually comes at the beginning of the paragraph.**

**Read the paragraphs below. Underline the topic sentence in each paragraph. Then write the topic sentence on the lines below each paragraph.**

We live in a salty world. There is salt on earth and in the oceans. Inside of you there is salt. It is in your blood, sweat, and tears. It's a good thing, because without salt you would die.

_____

_____

The Blue Jay is not friendly with other birds. It eats the eggs of other birds. The Blue Jay also will eat baby birds. It is no wonder other birds don't like the Blue Jay.

_____

_____

Name _____

# The Topic Sentence

> Every paragraph has a main idea or topic sentence.
> This tells what the paragraph is about.
> The topic sentence usually comes at the beginning of the paragraph.

**Read the paragraphs below. Underline the topic sentence in each paragraph. Then write the topic sentence on the lines below each paragraph.**

Giant ships with sails are called clippers. The Red Jacket was a famous ocean clipper. It sailed between New York and England. In 1854, it crossed the Atlantic in 13 days. That record has never been broken.

_____
_____

The last dinosaur died about 65 million years ago. No one knows why. One thought is that new kinds of plants began to grow. Some dinosaurs could not eat them and starved. Then there was no food for the meat-eating dinosaurs.

_____
_____

Writing Paragraphs         8         © 1983, 1996 Remedia Publications

Name _____

# Topic Sentences

**Write a complete topic sentence for each topic below.**

**EXAMPLE:** your favorite day      <u>My favorite day is Saturday.</u>

someone special _____
_____

hardest subject in school _____
_____

best subject in school _____
_____

an animal _____
_____

a sport _____
_____

a song _____
_____

your city _____
_____

**Pick one of the topic sentences you wrote. Write it on the lines below. Add one more complete sentence about the topic sentence.**

_____
_____
_____
_____
_____

Name _____

# Topic Sentences

Write a complete topic sentence for each topic below.

**EXAMPLE:** an airplane trip   <u>**I took an airplane trip to Washington D.C. last year.**</u>

winning a million dollars _____
_____

a trip to Disneyland _____
_____

being trapped in an elevator _____
_____

a banana split _____
_____

hitting a home run _____
_____

**Pick one of the topic sentences you wrote. Write it on the lines below. Add two more complete sentences about the topic sentence.**

_____
_____
_____
_____

Name _____

# Topic Sentences

**Write a complete topic sentence for each topic below.**

**EXAMPLE:** a favorite cartoon character    <u>**My favorite cartoon character is Snoopy.**</u>

first day of school _____
_____

Saturdays _____
_____

summer vacation _____
_____

a good athlete _____
_____

a favorite relative _____
_____

my best day _____
_____

my worst day _____
_____

**Pick one of the topic sentences you wrote. Write it on the lines below. Add two more complete sentences about the topic sentence.**

_____
_____
_____
_____

Name _____

# Topic Sentences

Write a complete topic sentence for each topic below.

**EXAMPLE:** a pet     <u>**I once had a snake for a pet.**</u>

a favorite TV program _____
_____

a special birthday _____
_____

a brother or sister _____
_____

a neat car _____
_____

favorite book _____
_____

favorite movie _____
_____


**Pick one of the topic sentences you wrote. Write it on the lines below. Add four more complete sentences about the topic sentence.**

_____
_____
_____
_____
_____
_____

Name _____

# Sentence Order

**The sentences in a paragraph must be in the correct order.**

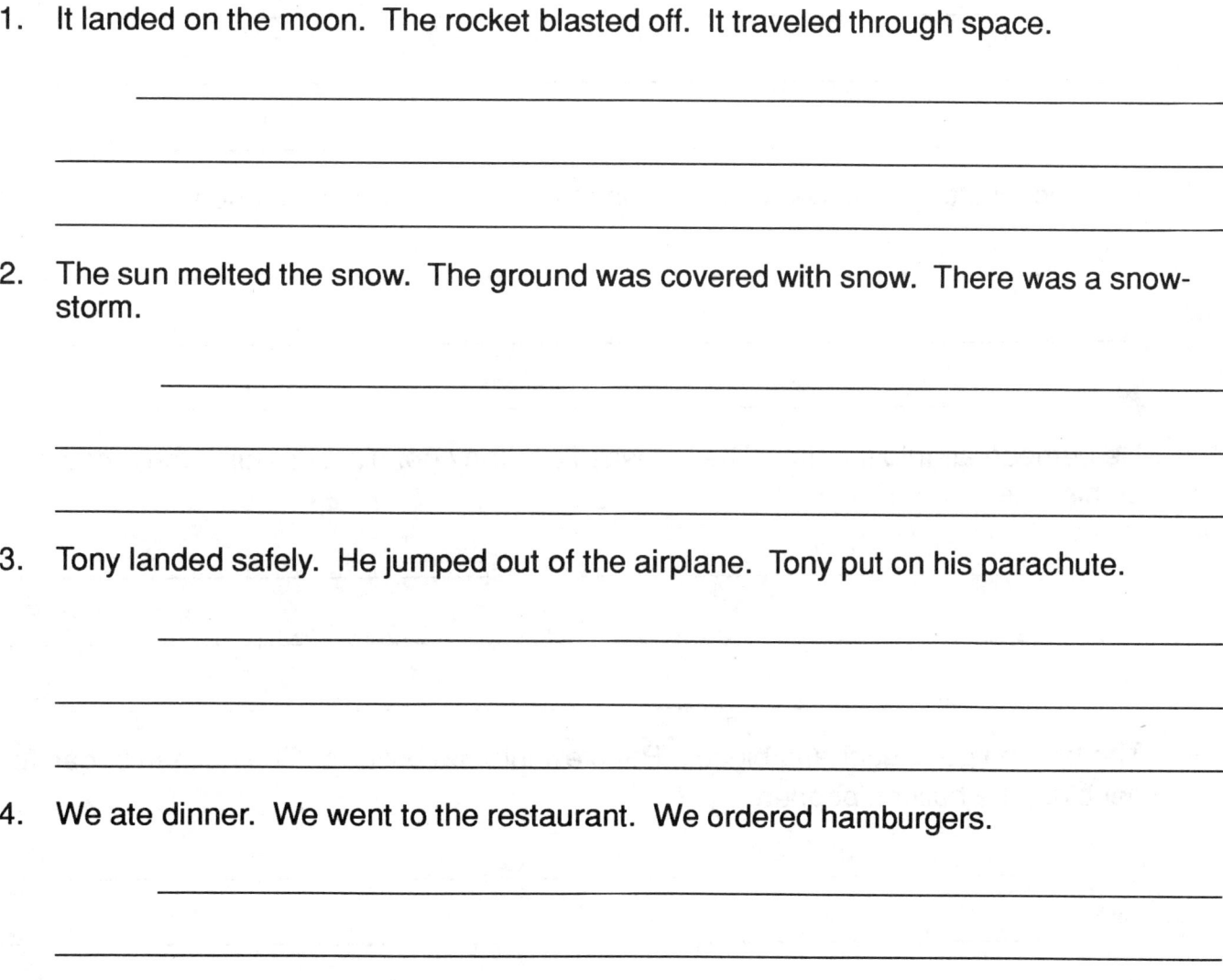

**This group of sentences is not in the correct order.**
   He pulled my tooth.  I went to the dentist.  I had a toothache.
**Now the sentences have been put in the correct order.**
   I had a toothache.  I went to the dentist.  He pulled my tooth.

**Write these groups of sentences in the correct order.**

1. It landed on the moon.  The rocket blasted off.  It traveled through space.

   _____

   _____

   _____

2. The sun melted the snow.  The ground was covered with snow.  There was a snowstorm.

   _____

   _____

   _____

3. Tony landed safely.  He jumped out of the airplane.  Tony put on his parachute.

   _____

   _____

   _____

4. We ate dinner.  We went to the restaurant.  We ordered hamburgers.

   _____

   _____

   _____

**Challenge:  Add two sentences to this topic sentence:**  The alarm clock rang.

Name _____

# Sentence Order

> **The sentences in a paragraph must be in the correct order.**

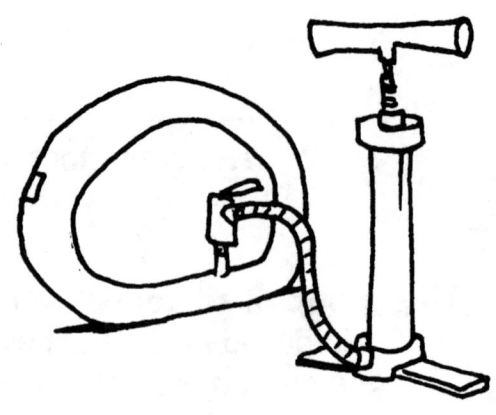

**Write these groups of sentences in the correct order.**

1. We won the game.  I hit a home run.  The score of the game was tied.

   _____
   _____
   _____

2. It rained all afternoon.  Dark clouds appeared.  We played in the puddles.

   _____
   _____
   _____

3. He pumped air into the tire.  The tire was flat.  Tony got his air pump.  Tony rode away on his bike.

   _____
   _____
   _____

4. The balloon got bigger and bigger.  Pat blew into the balloon.  The balloon began to get big.  The balloon popped.

   _____
   _____
   _____

Name _____

# Sentence Order

**The pictures and sentences below tell a story. They are not in the correct order. The story doesn't make sense.**

**Number each sentence from 1 to 4 to show the correct order for the story. The first sentence has been numbered for you.**

☐ He threw the line into the water.

[1] Tim put a worm on the fishhook.

☐ Then he cooked it.

☐ Tim caught a fish.

**Write the sentences to make the paragraph.**

_____
_____
_____
_____

**Make up a title for your paragraph.** _____

**Challenge: Add another sentence to your paragraph.**

© 1983, 1996 Remedia Publications     15     Writing Paragraphs

Name _____

# Sentence Order

The pictures and sentences below tell a story. They are not in the correct order. The story doesn't make sense.

**Number each sentence from 1 to 4 to show the correct order for the story.**

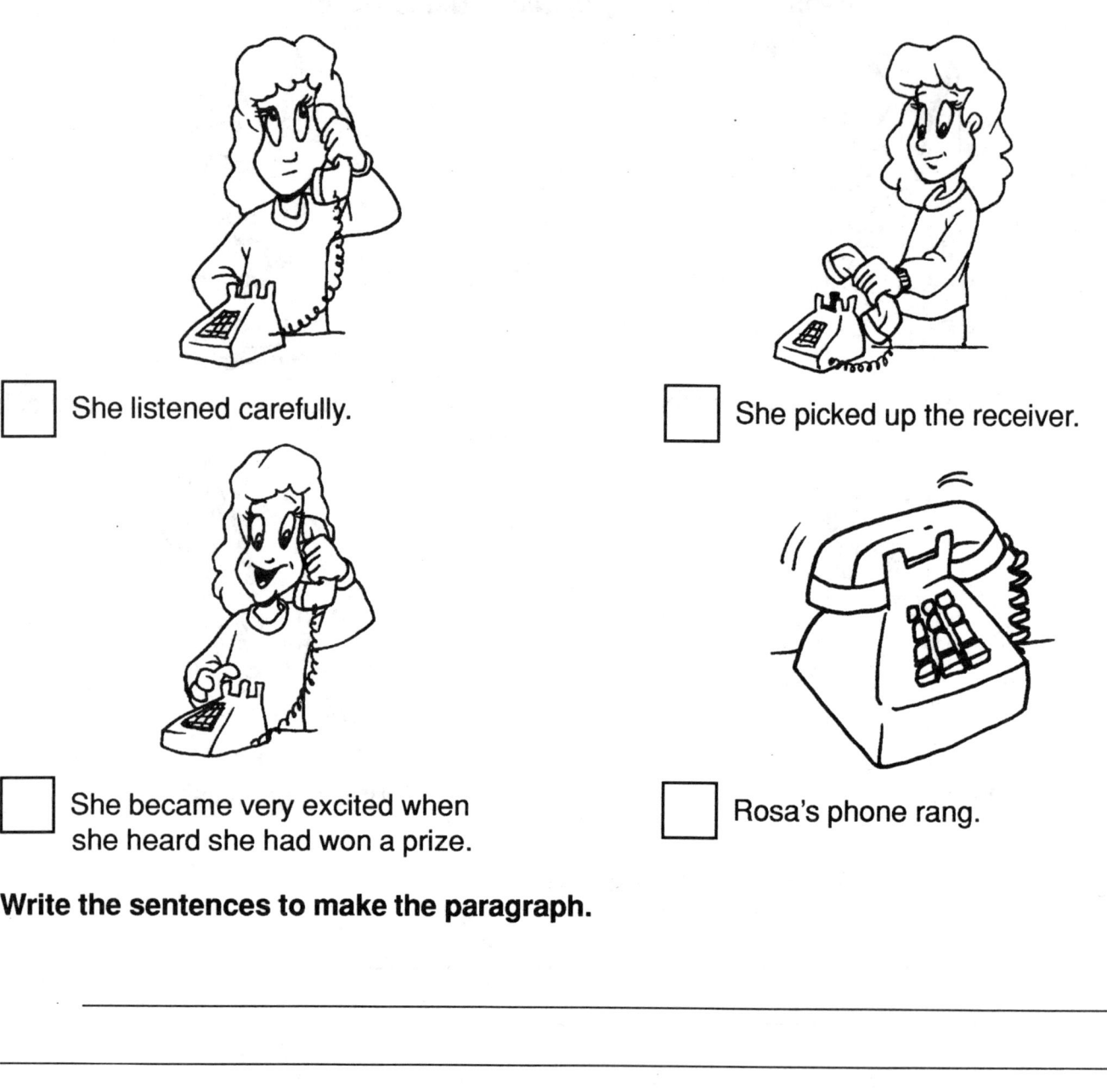

☐ She listened carefully.

☐ She picked up the receiver.

☐ She became very excited when she heard she had won a prize.

☐ Rosa's phone rang.

**Write the sentences to make the paragraph.**

_____
_____
_____
_____

**Make up a title for your paragraph.** _____

Name _____

# Developing a Paragraph

> The first sentence in a paragraph usually tells the main idea or topic of the paragraph. It is called the topic sentence. THE OTHER SENTENCES TELL MORE ABOUT THE TOPIC SENTENCE.

Write a paragraph about EATING POPCORN. The topic sentence has been done for you. Write at least four complete sentences about the topic sentence.

Use the ideas in the box to help you.

**POPCORN**

| | |
|---|---|
| How does it look? | puffy, white, yellow from butter |
| How does it feel? | warm, light, soft as it's chewed |
| How does it smell? | like butter, warm oil |
| How does it sound? | crunchy when you bite it |
| How does it taste? | buttery, salty, delicious |

*Eating popcorn is a treat.*

_____
_____
_____
_____
_____
_____

**Challenge:** Write four sentences describing what it's like to eat a bowl of ice cream.

Name _____

# Developing a Paragraph

Write a paragraph about EATING AN APPLE. The topic sentence has been done for you. Write at least four complete sentences about the topic sentence.

Use the ideas in the box to help you.

**AN APPLE**

| | |
|---|---|
| How does it look? | shiny, smooth, round, fresh |
| How does it smell? | delicious, sweet, fresh |
| How does it sound? | crunchy when you bite it |
| How does it taste? | sweet, tart, sometimes sour |

*Eating a big, red apple is something I really enjoy.*

_____
_____
_____
_____
_____

**Challenge:** Think of one of your favorite foods. Write a paragraph describing what it is like to eat that food.

Writing Paragraphs

Name _____

# Developing a Paragraph

Add two complete sentences to each topic sentence below. Be sure the sentences tell more about the topic sentence.

**EXAMPLE:** Last night I walked into a dark, haunted house. <u>I heard strange noises. Suddenly a hand reached out and touched me.</u>

<u>One night there was a thunderstorm.</u>
_____
_____
_____
_____

<u>I went up in a spacecraft with an astronaut.</u>
_____
_____
_____
_____

<u>Once I got really mad.</u>
_____
_____
_____
_____

**CHALLENGE:** Choose one of the paragraphs above. On a separate sheet of paper, rewrite the paragraph and add two sentences to it.

Name _____

# Developing a Paragraph

Add three complete sentences to each topic sentence below. Be sure the sentences tell more about the topic sentence.

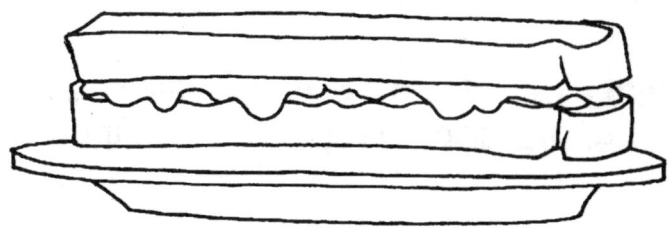

*I know how to make a peanut butter and jelly sandwich.*
*First* _____
_____
_____
_____

*I know how to make a jack-o-lantern. First* _____
_____
_____
_____

*I know how to plant a garden. First* _____
_____
_____
_____

**CHALLENGE:** Write a paragraph explaining how to clean your room.

Name _____

# Developing a Paragraph

**Add four complete sentences to each topic sentence below. Be sure the sentences tell more about the topic sentence.**

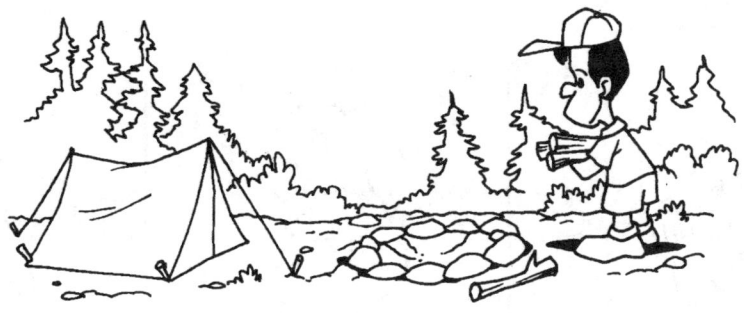

*I know how to build a campfire. First* _____
_____
_____
_____
_____

*I know how to wash a car. First* _____
_____
_____
_____
_____

**CHALLENGE:** Write a paragraph explaining how to fly a kite.

Name _____

# Developing a Paragraph

**Look at the pictures. They tell a story. On the lines below the pictures, add three complete sentences to the topic sentence which has already been done for you.**

_____

*Ted had a bad day at school today.*
_____
_____
_____
_____
_____
_____
_____

**Make up a title for your paragraph.**

**CHALLENGE:** Add two more sentences to your paragraph.

Name _____

# Developing a Paragraph

**Look at the pictures. They tell a story. Write sentences to tell the story. Start with a topic sentence. Then add three complete sentences to the topic sentence.**

_____

(topic sentence) _____
_____
_____
_____
_____
_____
_____
_____

**Make up a title for your paragraph.**

**CHALLENGE: Add two more sentences to your paragraph.**

Name _____

# Developing a Paragraph

Write a paragraph that describes this picture. Start with a topic sentence that tells what the paragraph is going to be about. Add at least four complete sentences to your topic sentence.

_____

(topic sentence)_____

_____
_____
_____
_____
_____
_____
_____

**Make up a title for your paragraph.**

Writing Paragraphs           24           © 1983, 1996 Remedia Publications

Name _____

# Developing a Paragraph

**Write a paragraph that describes this picture. Start with a topic sentence that tells what the paragraph is going to be about. Add at least four complete sentences to your topic sentence.**

(topic sentence) _____
_____
_____
_____
_____
_____
_____
_____
_____

**CHALLENGE: Write a paragraph about two girls making a deluxe pizza.**

Name _____

# Developing a Paragraph

**Write a paragraph that describes this picture. Start with a topic sentence that tells what the paragraph is going to be about. Add at least four complete sentences to your topic sentence.**

_____

(topic sentence) _____

_____
_____
_____
_____
_____
_____
_____

**Make up a title for your paragraph.**

**Challenge:** Write a paragraph describing what happens after the robbers are caught or they escape.

Name _____

# Developing a Paragraph

Imagine that you must write a commercial to read on the radio. You may choose one of the ideas from the Idea Box. Be sure to include the following information in your commercial:

1. Introduction
2. Name of the product
3. Special features
4. Why someone should buy it
5. Where you can get it
6. How much it costs
7. Ending

**IDEA BOX**

1. a hat that makes you invisible
2. a bike that turns into a boat

_____
_____
_____
_____
_____
_____
_____
_____
_____
_____
_____
_____
_____

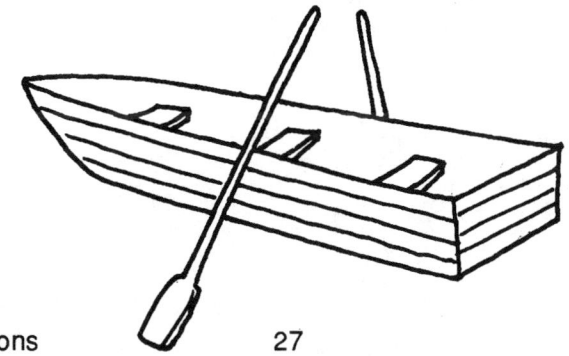

Name _____

# Developing a Paragraph

**Imagine that you must write an introduction for someone. Choose one of the names from the Idea box. Tell some interesting details about that person. Have at least five sentences in your paragraph. (You may have to do a little research.)**

| IDEA BOX | |
|---|---|
| John F. Kennedy | Little Miss Muffet |
| one of your parents | Neil Armstrong |
| Mr. Rogers | Madame Curie |
| Abraham Lincoln | Pinocchio |
| Elvis Presley | Charles Lindbergh |
| Thomas Edison | Miss Piggy |

*I'd like to introduce* _____

_____
_____
_____
_____
_____
_____
_____
_____
_____
_____

# Developing a Paragraph

**Write a paragraph about a historical event. You may choose one of the ideas from the Idea Box. Have at least six sentences in your paragraph. (You may have to do some research.)**

**IDEA BOX**

Eruption of Mt. Vesuvius
Sinking of the Titanic
John Glenn orbits the earth
Wright Brothers invent the airplane
Midnight ride of Paul Revere
Building of pyramids in Egypt

Name _____

# Developing a Paragraph

**Write a paragraph about an important invention. You may choose one of the ideas from the Idea Box. Have at least six sentences in your paragraph. (You may have to do some research.)**

**IDEA BOX**

Invention of the first motor car
Invention of the printing press
Invention of the first hot air balloon
Invention of the telephone
Invention of the television
Invention of gunpowder

Writing Paragraphs